JAMIE

CW00394248

GOD DOESN'T DO MAGIC

The transforming power of process

A POWERFUL STORY OF FREEDOM FROM
CRIPPLING ANXIETY

With Rachel Lee

Published in the United Kingdom by Dream Revolution Publishing.

ISNB 978-1-8380856-0-5

Cover Design: Rachel Lee

Preface

Trust is always the way home. Since coming to Christ - age 18, I have been on this amazing journey of letting go of my own anxious thoughts and trusting God's liberating thoughts for me. This book describes the process; a tried and tested map home to peace and how I discovered it. It is the result of a number of talks given between 2017-20 on the same subject.

The expression *God doesn't do magic* is borrowed from Graham Cooke.

Thanks

Some concepts and terminology found in his book are indebted to the work of a number of thinkers and writers. I am grateful for their insights and inspiration. Although not always able to quote them directly, you will find our sources at the back of this book.

I am also very thankful for our friends Patrick Mayfield and David Pike who have provided valuable insights and corrections on this book.

Disclaimer

This book is meant to inspire you to go on your own journey of freedom. It will give you an in-depth insight on how process is needed to break the cycle of negative emotions such as anxiety and OCD. It will help you by providing tools to break strongholds and renew your mind in Jesus-Christ. However, I am not a doctor or a therapist. So, please do not quit medications or treatments without the advice of your professional health carer.

Table of Contents

Why this book?

"The church is full of people who have been touched but not changed… Transformation can only happen through the renewing of the mind." - Graham Cooke

"I'm telling you, these walls are funny. First you hate 'em, then you get used to 'em. Enough time passes, you get so you depend on them. That's institutionalised." - 'The Shawshank Redemption', (Film,1995)

In Michael Singer's Untethered Soul, there is a story about a man with a thorn in his arm: rather than embrace the pain of extracting the thorn, he built a protective shield to protect it from being bumped. It never occurred to him that it might be easier, simpler, and more liberating to remove the thorn.

We can find ourselves in the same situation as this man. We might long to see the 'thorn' of our anxiety, fear, anger, disappointment and rejection removed, but then wince at the thought of its removal. Rather than truly embrace the emotional pain of the transformation process for our freedom, we too, carefully construct boxes to protect ourselves from being knocked and settle for managing or covering up our strongholds.

Here's the thing: the Cross of Christ is the decisive victory. Instantly, through Jesus, we become glorious in the sight of God. The Father sees each believer as worthy, striking, beautiful, celebrated, marvellous, wonderful, excellent, unforgettable, and distinguished. As Christians, we are not peeling layers in order to be more and more acceptable in His eyes; we have fundamentally been made right and we are accepted and loved by God. His Spirit lives in us and empowers us to live a new life in a new land.

However, into this new country, we often bring with us some of our old stuff; though made new, most of us continue with old bad habits and practices we have learnt in order to numb our pain, avoid responsibility and feel safe.

God's ultimate dream for our lives is freedom. Freedom allows us to live full of passion, energy and life! Freedom fires up our imagination and creativity. Freedom means to be fully present in the moment, able to be honest, authentic and seen; no longer crushed by the crippling weight of guilt, shame, and perfectionism.

God doesn't do magic is about accepting that this kind of freedom rarely comes instantaneously but through a gradual, sometimes painful, unsettling transformative process that involves stepping out into the unknown without self-protection. It is written to help you understand what is your part and what is God's part in the deconstruction process of your strongholds, so that you would live in the freedom God promised through Jesus Christ. Christ has set us free to live a free life (Galatians 5:1, The Message translation).

The inspiration behind this book is my own story of progressively journeying out of Obsessive, Compulsive, Disorder (OCD) and the revelation that I had built my own prison walls in order to feel safe and cope with my pain. It's also the story of how I learnt to hate the imprisoning walls enough to be willing to embark upon the initially unsettling journey into freedom with God.

My story

"A thought is harmless unless we believe it." - Byron Katie

For most of my life, I have struggled with "doubting disease", also know as OCD. It started when I was 11 years old. In order to feel safe, I developed a complex ritual of lengthy, anxious checking routines.

Did I lock the door properly? Did I turn off the taps? I was fearful about making a mistake that would be the cause of something bad to happen. I feared that I could miss something that could somehow lead to a fire, a flood, or theft.

When I became a Christian, this mindset didn't just suddenly disappear. In fact, my anxiety intensified as I believed I could now do something to offend God. Would I think, say, or do something wrong that displeased him which resulted in punishment? My mind became increasing ruled by terrible accusations and I lived dominated by harsh internal critical chatter.

As the outward visible checking of doors and taps being closed etc. continued, this internal critical voice plagued me with accusations and false guilt, ultimately resulting in the development of a whole new set of hidden internal checking routines articulated around performance, motivation and responsibility.

The most debilitating and crippling aspect of OCD, was the fear that something I imagined could actually have happened. These obsessive thoughts became so intrusive that they tormented me to think that the worst case scenario had happened or would happen because of my failure. I found myself in a grip of excessive worry that could only be appeased by generating these new unseen mental routines.

For years, I was haunted by tormenting internal monologues and stabbing thoughts caused by a cruel, harsh and critical inner voice. I lived every day under the lie "if you feel guilty then you are guilty". As a consequence, I became a slave to the obsessive checking routines and rituals that I had constructed for my own safety.

I felt at times I was losing my mind. The intrusive thoughts disrupted many amazing and ordinary moments, resulting in foggy confusion, and impaired reasoning. When facing even the slightest temptation, false guilt would overwhelm me. I would also constantly replay conversations in my head to search for my mistakes. I would digress, retreat to obsess, and scrutinise the accusation. Was it true? Was this truly my motivation? A habitual mental loop was engaged in order to ascertain if the accusation was correct or not.

I longed for peace of mind. I longed to leave the prison of my thoughts. On one hand, I hated the rituals and the checking routines, yet I enjoyed the secondary benefits they provided. The whole mechanism was underpinned by the lie that checking would provide me with the peace and rest I needed, but this false peace was always temporary. Like Red, played by Morgan Freeman in "The Shawshank Redemption", I hated the walls and at the same time depended upon them. The compulsive checking gave me a sense of control and false well-being.

God doesn't do magic

"Satan always sends error into the world in pairs that are opposites. His great hope is that you will get so upset about one of his errors, that you'll react into the opposite one, and he's got you." - C.S. Lewis

It is interesting to notice that often, our strengths and weaknesses are not so far apart. In the same way, I could develop a negative obsession, I relentlessly started to pursue the question of how change does happen.

How could such a powerful, debilitating mindset be torn down? What is my part and what is God's part? Who smashes the carefully constructed box? Is it something God does for me, or is it entirely up to me?

The reason I wrestled for years with this question was because I didn't like the answer I found. I longed for God to do magic, to just zap me out of confusion. Many times I had experienced the sudden breakthrough of God where the demonic oppression was clearly broken. However, whilst I was having significant supernatural encounters, these weren't producing the lasting liberty I was so desperate to enjoy. It is easy for God to cast off a spirit but God does not cast out a mindset and zap us into the promise land of freedom.

Over time I came to understand that without changing how I think, I could be powerfully touched by God, but not transformed. Getting free and staying free are two very different things. There isn't an impartation of transformation that replaces my responsibility to choose my thoughts. To enjoy freedom, I still had to renew my mind, take thoughts captive and see my thinking gradually transformed.

The discovery that I had a part to play in my own freedom came with its own set of challenges. As C.S. Lewis said, Satan always sends error and distraction in pairs of opposites. He does not mind which one you choose as long as you go to one extreme or the other: either extreme passivity, "I live in a carefully constructed box and if God wants me out, he can do the magic and zap me out Himself"; or "it's all just about me, my discipline, my practices, my habits and my determination".

So for years, I found myself oscillating between these two extremes. On one hand, sheer will power, drivenness to change, and on the other passively waiting for God to magically zap me into His promised freedom.

I became a practitioner of me-ology where by through navel gazing and introspection, I strove to discover my broken spots. I obsessively pursued self-discipline and behaviour-modification where I attempted to transform myself through gritted teeth, white knuckles and will power. The problem was that going to the extreme of self-awareness only produced in me neurotic suffering, pain and misery. Struggle should always cause us to first look upwards to God and not inwards. Freedom is not a rallying call to pull up your socks, grit your teeth and try harder, nor is it an invitation to be a passive victim.

My striving itself also became a form of numbing. It was easier to cover up my fears and my struggles by busying myself. Striving and working for freedom stopped me from facing how really enslaved I was. Rest became impossible, as it was in silence and stillness that the accusing chatter was at its loudest.

My part, God's part

"Don't copy the behaviour and customs of this world, but let God transform you into a new person by changing the way you think" - Romans 12:2, New Living Translation (NLT)

Freedom always comes from two sides. First, there's God's initiative, His sovereign gracious intervention. In those moments of revelation, we get woken up by God. Like Paul we have encounters where we get knocked off our donkey (Acts 9:4); times where we come to know what we previously didn't know. God speaks, and our spiritual eyes get opened; we are given an invitation to walk in a fresh perspective. But that's not the end of the story. Divine intervention doesn't make freedom inevitable. Our response is needed too: our yes, our actions, are the second vital part of this process.

In the life of Joshua, we can see the interaction between God's sovereign gracious gift and personal resolve cooperating.

Deuteronomy 34:9 says that Moses laid his hands on Joshua and he was filled with the spirit of wisdom. Joshua got an impartation of wisdom; he got something he didn't earn, or strive to make happen. It was a gift of grace. But that impartation of wisdom did not bring Joshua into a life of passivity and irresponsibility. He was also instructed to be brave, to choose courage and to meditate on God's promises, not allowing discouragement to rest over his soul like an oppressive blanket (Joshua 1:8).

Joshua did not lead the people into the Promised Land by watching and waiting for God to sprinkle fairy dust and zap them into their inheritance. He got them into the land by embracing these two realities: looking for God's strategy and power, whilst at the same time taking personal responsibility to renew his mind. God had reminded him of the things he could do, the practices or habits he could embrace in order to make his own way prosperous and successful. In other words, God was saying to Joshua "Joshua you are a lot more powerful than you realise!".

Encounters with God invite us into a process, a journey of changing the way we think. In this process, we choose to let go of a passive victim mentality and start to believe that we can co-labour, co-operate and cultivate what we have received. What God does in a sudden sovereign encounter, requires us to work together with Him in process.

We do it together

"Before you trust, you have to listen" - Romans 10:17, The Message (MSG)

The process invites us into an opportunity to learn about God, his dependability, faithfulness, and His trustworthiness. In process with God, we discover that God is kind, reliable and good. The process allows us to get to know Him personally.

I came to realise that smashing the carefully constructed box of OCD was much more like sailing than being zapped into liberty. There's the anticipation of the wind of the Holy Spirit blowing in my sails, enjoying the expectation of freeing revelation coming at any point, at a conference, through a film, a book, a scripture, an impartation, a testimony. Then once the sails are full, it's about the personal decision to tack into the wind, adjusting in order to co-operate with the momentum that comes from the revelation. In other words, I wasn't on my own trying to change myself; rather, God was continuously active in my will (Philippians 2:13). Then in order to walk in freedom, I had to make the decision to cultivate and co-operate with His working. The greatest asset we have is our mind, and whatever gets our minds, gets us.

How to spot a stronghold?

"For *as a man thinks in his heart, so is he.*" - Proverbs 23:7, New King James Version (NKJV)

The ultimate goal of renewing our mind is to come to a place of joyful, trusting reliance upon God. Everything changes for us, the moment we believe, trust and have faith. Something that might have plagued our mind for years can shift in an instant! Trust is the crucial transforming weapon. Everything is ultimately about relaxing in His loving leadership.

Trust is what liberates us from being obsessed with ourselves. When I saw that the lack of trust in God was at the root of my pain, I was face to face with the source of my internal conflict. I wasn't a victim: the root of my struggles was independence. I kept in control and designed my own checking mechanisms in order to keep a sense of false peace. Bottom line: I trusted my rituals because I didn't trust God.

It was my self-trust that was restricting, and holding me back. In order to be free, I simply needed to change the way I thought. It is the belief that I needed rituals in order to be safe that kept me enslaved to checking. It would be the belief that I was secure, held onto by God that would make my obsessive compulsions immediately redundant.

However, embracing trust is simpler said than done. Standing between me and the lived-out freedom were pockets of enemy resistance - a fortified area controlled by the enemy in my thinking. The stronghold formed, influenced and defended many of my false conclusions, ideas and thoughts. For years, I had placed a huge amount of confidence in the enemy's arguments and reasoning. I had trusted the idea that I was only really safe and secure from blame, judgment and punishment if I looked after myself. I believed my own thoughts, and stubbornly refused to trust God's. My 'stinking thinking' was the source of my turmoil and freedom was only possible if I changed my mind. This was the revelation that God was steadily birthing in my will; this was the truth that would catapult me from being a victim to being an overcomer.

Freedom comes as you demolish strongholds and build new ones through changing your mind about what you trust to be true. A stronghold could be described as a mental block, a blind-spot that stops you seeing things the way God sees them; an area of thinking that doesn't yet line up with how God, thinks and concludes. They are thoughts that are not yet yielding to God; thoughts that stop you reasoning, seeing and concluding in any other way.

A stronghold can be spotted by asking yourself the question "What story am I always telling myself about my present, past or future?" Or, as Wendy Backlund says, "What am I always trying to prove?" With OCD, I was obsessively trying to prove that I was safe, and that I wouldn't suffer loss. This stronghold produced in me a pre-occupation with danger, seeing threat absolutely everywhere. Fear, worry, anxiety operated in my imagination, fuelled by the speculation "What if?".

Strongholds can be formed by an identity founded upon something other than God's love. For example, comparison, competition, perfectionism are all performance-based strongholds. Strongholds influence us to intensely protect opportunities that promise significance, value and worth independently from God. They fuel the illusion that we are competent to run our own lives. Insecurity rooted in unworthiness can, for example, result in comparison, the fear of others more gifted than us, shame, competition, perfectionism, self-centredness - are all desperate attempts to find meaning, safety and value without God.

Another way to spot a stronghold is to question the fruit these thoughts are producing - or to ask ourselves: "What would I be experiencing right now without that thought?" We need to challenge every thought that doesn't produce peace, hope, joy and love. We are invited by Holy Spirit to change our mind, and reject any thoughts that rob us of our confidence regarding who we are in Christ. We need to tear down any belief that contradicts God's assessment of our value, worth and identity. Our preoccupation needs to be what has God said, who has God called us to be, what is our status in His eyes, what He says about our past, present and future?

Brick by brick, stone by stone

"Timothy, my son, I am giving you this command in keeping with the prophecies once made about you, so that by recalling them you may fight the battle well." - 1 Timothy 1:18, New International Version (NIV)

Demolishing a stronghold is taking captive any argument or conclusion that contradicts who God says He is and who He says you are. Taking thoughts captive requires us to change the story we listen or listened to; it demands time and process.

Generally, a stronghold wasn't built in a day, rather it was established brick by brick, thought by thought, day after day, learning to see life through a particular lens and organising your thoughts according to a particular story. According to the National Science Foundation, the mind thinks between 12,000 to 60,000 thoughts a day on average, and 95% of those thoughts are repetitive subconscious self-talk. Experts have also found that

80% of our thoughts are negative, which could amount up to 48,000 negative thoughts a day, with those thoughts patterns being repeated on a daily basis.

The birthplace of the blind spot or negative self-talk might have been critical words or an emotionally charged event. Someone significant may have rejected you, or introduced fear into your life. Afterwards, the action, the event or the words are revisited, reviewed, mulled over, and reimagined - like a movie we watch in our mind's eye. Fear can even become a stronghold through watching an emotionally-charged television show. I remember becoming absolutely terrified, traumatised by the thought of becoming blind after watching the episodes of 'Little House On The Prairie' where Mary Ingalls goes blind (yes, I know - you're smiling!) Reimagining, reviewing and thinking about theses episodes created a stronghold that gave the enemy influence.

Negative strongholds produce a great deal of pain, and pain is not pleasant. We want it to be over now. Instead of embracing the process of tearing down a stronghold, we get stuck looking for quick fixes and easy solutions. Instead of co-labouring, we hope for God to suddenly take over and do it for us. My repetitive prayers were: "Help me now, I'm hurting, take away the pain, please switch off my mind". Of course, God listened to and cared about every single one of these prayers. However, because He is most passionate about relationship, He didn't answer them by doing magic, sprinkling fairy dust and zapping me out of these unwanted mindsets. It would be through the process of gradual transformation that I would get to know Him and trust Him. Whilst he was neither the author, nor the source or architect of my pain, God wasn't in a rush to get me out of debilitating OCD. Pain had to do its job first.

The power of practices

"For it is God who works in you to will and to act in order to fulfil His good purpose." - Philippians 2:13, New International Version (NIV)

God promises to lead guide, direct and keep us on track (Proverbs 3:5-6). He is committed to work powerfully in our will. But there are things we can prioritise that cause us to lean into His promise to be at work.

For example, I found that freedom gradually came as I gave myself to the following disciplines:

- Being in His Word everyday. Trusting His promises and his words to be a cutting sword (Hebrews 4:12).
- Giving time to being in God's presence. We are transformed when we contemplate the Lord's glory in worship and prayerful meditation (2 Corinthians 3:18).

- Walking deeply with others. Authentic relationships are a beautiful provision and safeguard, God promises that the slap of a friend is beneficial (Proverbs 27:6).
- Becoming a student of your own words. Out of the overflow of the heart the mouth speaks. Our words give us wonderfully clear insights into our subconscious beliefs (Matthew 12:23-24, Luke 6:45, Proverbs 4:23).

These practices positioned me to catch the wind, and co-operate with His work in me. Through them, God was constantly dropping gifts of grace in my life. They were invitations to repent and change the way I think (Romans 12:2).

So our part is to co-operate with His activity in our will; to form fresh outlooks, attitudes, and conclusions in line with His activity at the core of who we are. Once we have revelation of God's activity upon our will, we are then free to decide an "intelligent application" (as Dallas Willard calls it) of what God is willing in us. In others words, we practically look at what repentance, changing the way we think looks like in reality. Revelation gives us power to initiate change.

2 Corinthians 10:3-6 tells us that we have weapons with divine power to demolish these beliefs, arguments, speculations and conclusions. We have the capacity, through co-labouring with God's working in us, to construct new ways of seeing and acting. If a negative way of seeing was established through repetition, likewise, a positive one will be built through practices that we repeat. If habits imprisoned us, godly habits are going to get us out. Planned disciplines will enable us to cultivate brand new thoughts, actions, words and behaviour.

Knowing me - knowing you!

"Every issue in your life was designed to be solved through a trusting connection with Father." - Danny Silk

"When you are in the fight for your life approach the battle as simply as possible. Believing simply that God is good and you are a much loved child." - Graham Cooke

Two revelations became critical for me in tearing the stronghold down.

The first was knowing God as a good Father. God informed my heart that He is the one who sees me, intimately knows me and loves me unconditionally. Freedom was ultimately found in trusting His loving leadership. Through a growing intimate connection with God, I heard His words break through my many layers of self protection: "I will instruct you and teach you in the way you should go; I will counsel you with my loving eye on you" (Psalm 32:8). He kept reminding me that His attention doesn't switch on and off, that He is constantly attentive and fiercely protective of me (Psalm 23).

The second revelation was that how I responded to His affection was key in tearing down the stronghold that was oppressing me. Did I want freedom enough that I was willing to let Him love me, lead me and subsequently transform me?

Repentance is not an emotion

"They're strange things, consciences. Trouble is, what feels best isn't necessarily what works best." - 'Denial' (Film, 2016)

When you have trusted yourself for decades, trusting another to work on your behalf can be an emotionally difficult decision. I came to understand that if I wanted to enjoy real peace, I would have to take the daily cold-blooded decision to trust Him to lead. If I waited for a feeling of "it is safe to trust", it simply was never going to happen.

The starting point of repentance is often the cold blooded decision to trust and obey. Graham Cooke teaches that the WILL seldom becomes activated into action through feelings or emotions. We must decide not to let our emotions run the show. Emotions eventually come into line with what we actively will and decide to do. Emotions are not designed to lead. We sometimes get stuck in our growth because of the reality that spiritual growth and comfort don't initially go together. Change can be an emotionally painful experience. Growth feels good after, rarely during. Liberty feels good afterwards, but not in the middle of the process.

To walk into freedom, we need to come to believe "God said it! I believe it! That settles it!" This requires a kind of death, surrender and yielding (John 12:24).

The point of surrender is not an easy place to come to. We tend to believe thoughts that have the strongest emotions attached to them: "if it feels true then it is true!" Initially, it can feel vulnerable unsafe and even dangerous to trust and agree with God. However, freedom only comes as we daily take the cold-blooded decision to not settle for the emotional comfort the stronghold provides.

This cold-blooded determination is well illustrated in 'The Greatest Showman' song "from now on": *"From Now On, What's waited until tomorrow starts tonight. One day is today. One day is right now."*. That carefully constructed box is going to be demolished, starting now! There must be this resolve to say enough is enough. As Rob Bell put it: *"… There is renewal, freedom when you come to the end of your own power and strength… A moment where you stop and say "This isn't working, I'm exhausted, I'm tired of carrying this thing around. Here! God you take it!" It's at this point of surrender that things get really interesting…"* ('Oprah's SuperSoul Conversations', Podcast, April 22 2019.)

Finding a way through, not a way out

"I've had hundreds of people tell me what they don't want to feel: "I don't want to try because I don't want to feel disappointed" or "I just want this feeling to go away". "I understand", I said to them, "but you have dead peoples' goals. Only dead people don't get unwanted emotions or inconvenienced by their feelings. Only dead people never get stressed, never get broken hearts and never experience the disappointment that comes with failure. Tough emotions are part of our contract with life. You don't get to have a meaningful career, or raise a family, or leave the world a better place without stress and discomfort. Discomfort is the price of admission to a meaningful life"." - Susan David, 'The Gift and Power of Emotional Courage', Ted Talk, November 2017.

Thoughts need to be arrested, conquered, brought into submission and replaced with new ones (2 Corinthians 10:5). It's important to understand that some thoughts will go easily, whilst others are incredibly resistant. Changing a belief can be a violent thing. It can look like hacking through the jungle with a machete; it's finding a way through to new thoughts not just wanting to get out of pain.

Changing our mind can also be agony. There is discomfort in choosing to believe something that feels contradictory to the way you see life. It takes time to undo a mindset. Our part is to believe; take things captive; and walk, talk and fight according to the things that God has said. We are powerful and free, we can choose courage, we can choose to think about what God has said. Like Joshua, we can make our own way prosperous and successful.

Whilst I couldn't prevent unwanted thoughts popping into my head, I could choose what I did with them. I decided that it was ok to notice them, but I didn't need to be terrified of them, and fight to drop, or escape from them. I didn't need to be frightened by the uncertainty and insecurity they carried. I could choose in those moments to simply trust in Father God's leadership.

The tools of the trade

"God made us: invented us as a man invents an engine. A car is made to run on petrol, and it would not run properly on anything else. Now God designed the human machine to run on Himself. He Himself is the fuel our spirits were designed to burn, or the food our spirits were designed to feed on." - C.S. Lewis, 'Mere Christianity'

To get God's thoughts and God's story into our head we need practices, resolutions, things we do over and over again: daily habits, biblical meditation, memorisation, declarations etc. - any practices that cause us to run on God.

We constantly need to re-visit, and reimagine God's good thoughts. This is how we fix our thoughts on what is true. It is the truth that sets us free. Ask yourself: "What do I specifically need to believe to change how I think in this area?"; "What do I need to hear everyday in order to have another thought?".

What we constantly hear, we believe. What we say over ourselves becomes our reality. Those new thoughts and words are the bricks that make up a new positive stronghold.

This isn't behaviour modification or transformation by our own effort, we do this by God's grace. Practices and habits, and disciplines are tools, means of grace to access God's empowerment for transformation.

2 Thessalonians 1.11-12 (ESV) is a great explanation of this dynamic interactive process between us and God: "To this end we always pray for you, that our God may make you worthy of his calling and may fulfil every resolve for good and every work of faith by his power." Our confidence is not in our own discipline or will-power as if we were pulling ourselves up; rather, our expectation is in God's power working in our life as we engage in resolutions and the work of faith. It's about expecting God to be doing something powerful through these daily practices. It's about our expectation whilst engaging in a practice that connects us to His transformative power.

It's recognising that God's power is the decisive agent behind our experiential liberty and freedom. Our contribution is our resolve to cultivate some things and let go of others. The practices, habits and resolutions we develop are like the cable through which the transforming, liberating power of God travels.

Closing thoughts

"I find I'm so excited, I can barely sit still or hold a thought in my head. I think it is the excitement only a free man can feel, a free man at the start of a long journey whose conclusion is uncertain." - 'The Shawshank Redemption', Film, 1995

Be kind and compassionate with yourself on the journey. Sometimes I still find myself in the middle of an old familiar loop, using checking routines to frantically find false peace. I am still vulnerable to experiencing foreboding fear especially in times of joyful anticipation. My mind can easily tell me a story about fear of failure, future judgment and loss. I still have to be very careful about not giving room to the little foxes that spoil the vineyard. I have to be very suspicious of sudden intrusive thoughts that whisper "Go back and just check the lock once more. How can you relax if that door is left open?" A small thought like this, if entertained, is a doorway leading to much more chaotically debilitating thoughts.

But through my process with God, I now have a tried and tested map home to peace. When I get lost, I know how to get home: by simply inviting Jesus to be the 'umpire of my mind and to settle with finality the issue or controversy that has arisen in my thinking' - to paraphrase the words of Caroline Leaf. Trust is always the way home.

Brené Brown illustrates this process so well. When you are going somewhere you have never been before, you are probably going to get lost a couple of times. But if you go to that new place everyday for a month it's going to become easier like second nature. There comes a point where you can't even describe how you got there to someone else. It's automatic. God's thoughts, perspective, His narrative about our lives eventually become our natural default position.

We were born for freedom; freedom is our birthright. In the closing sequence of the film 'The Shawshank Redemption', Red expresses beautifully the wonder of freedom. Freedom beckons us to feel the excitement, of being fully alive. The only real question is, will we respond to God's magnificent invitation?

Sources

- Steve Backlund (2013), *Declarations: Unlocking Your Future*
- Wendy Backlund (2017), *Victorious Emotions: Creating a Framework for a Happier You*, Igniting Hope Ministries
- Brené Brown (2010), *The Gifts of Imperfection,* Publisher: Hazelden FIRM
- Byron Katie, *The work of Byron Katie, e-book,* https://thework.com/wp-content/uploads/2019/02/English_LB.pdf
- Graham Cooke (2016), *The way of the warrior Part 2*, MP3, iTunes.
- Graham Cooke, *God Doesn't Do Magic*, Brilliant perspectives.com, https://brilliantperspectives.com/god-doesnt-do-magic/
- Dawna Desilva, Teresa Liebscher (2016), *Sozo Saved Healed Delivered: A Journey into Freedom with the Father*, Son, and Holy Spirit, Destiny Image Publishers
- Benjamin Hardy (2020), *Personality Isn't Permanent: Break free from self-limiting beliefs and rewrite your story*, Portfolio
- Bill Johnson (2006), *When Heaven invades Earth*, Destiny Image Publishers

- Timothy Keller (2012), *The Freedom of Self Forgetfulness: The path to true Christian joy,* 10 Publishing
- Caroline Leaf (2015), *Switch On Your Brain*, Baker Books
- C. S. Lewis (2001), *Mere Christianity*, Harper, San Francisco
- Kristin Neff (2011), *Self-Compassion Step by Step: The Proven Power of Being Kind to Yourself,* Audio-book. https://www.audible.co.uk/pd/Self-Compassion-Step-by-Step-Audiobook/
- Kris Vallotton (2012), *Spirit Wars*, Chosen Books

About the Authors

Jamie and Rachel Lee are part of the leadership team of Church of Christ the King based in South East London. They are passionate about the city and impacting other Nations. They are also the creators of the Dream Revolution App. Their heart is to see people transformed by God's presence and completely free to live and dream big! Together they have two amazing daughters Fleur and Clémence. They absolutely love films, art, electronic music and food - the spicier the better!

Lightning Source UK Ltd.
Milton Keynes UK
UKHW022049141220
375052UK00012B/1092